POLINA'S DAY

To my father, who gave me my very first camera.

First published in Great Britain in 2001 by Frances Lincoln Limited,
4 Torriano Mews, Torriano Avenue, London NW5 2RZ

www.franceslincoln.com

First paperback edition 2003

British Library Cataloguing in Publication Data available on request

ISBN 0-7112-2122-7

Designed by Sophie Pelham

Printed in Singapore

1 3 5 7 9 8 6 4 2

AUTHOR ACKNOWLEDGEMENTS
With thanks to Polina Lesnevitch and her family for making this book possible.

POLINA'S DAY

From Dawn to Dusk in a Russian City

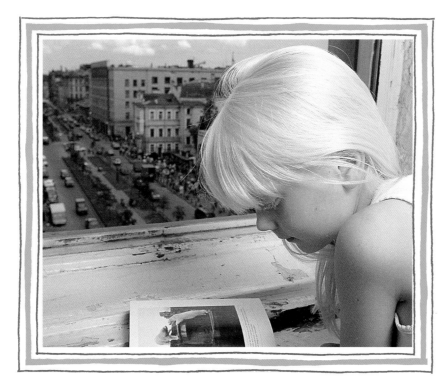

Andrey Ilyin

FRANCES LINCOLN

RUSSIA

St Petersburg

J274.183 £9.00

Polina and her family are 'Peterburdgets', the name given to people who live in Saint Petersburg. Saint Petersburg has played a very important role in Russia's history, and was our capital city for over 200 years (until Moscow took over this job in 1914).

Over the last century, Saint Petersburg has changed its name three times – from Saint Petersburg to Petrograd, to Leningrad, and then back to Saint Petersburg again – but it was originally named after Peter the Great, the Russian emperor who founded the city about 300 years ago. Peter described his new capital as a 'window on Europe' because of its unique position on the coast of the Baltic Sea, looking across to Europe.

Polina is a city girl: she lives in a high-rise apartment building and is used to lots of noise and traffic. But just like Russians everywhere, she has a very close-knit family. Both Polina's parents need to work full-time, but her grandparents live right next door and Polina spends time with them every day.

Polina is seven years old.
She lives with her parents
in a small flat on the 12th floor
of a 16-storey apartment block
in Saint Petersburg. Polina's
grandparents live in the flat
next door. Polina's mother,
Natalia, works as a cashier
at the local supermarket and
Polina's father, Alexey, is
a refrigerator mechanic.

As soon as she wakes up, Polina jumps out of bed and rushes to the shower. This is her favourite part of the morning and, even though her mother has called her for breakfast twice already, Polina's pretending she can't hear so she can carry on washing!

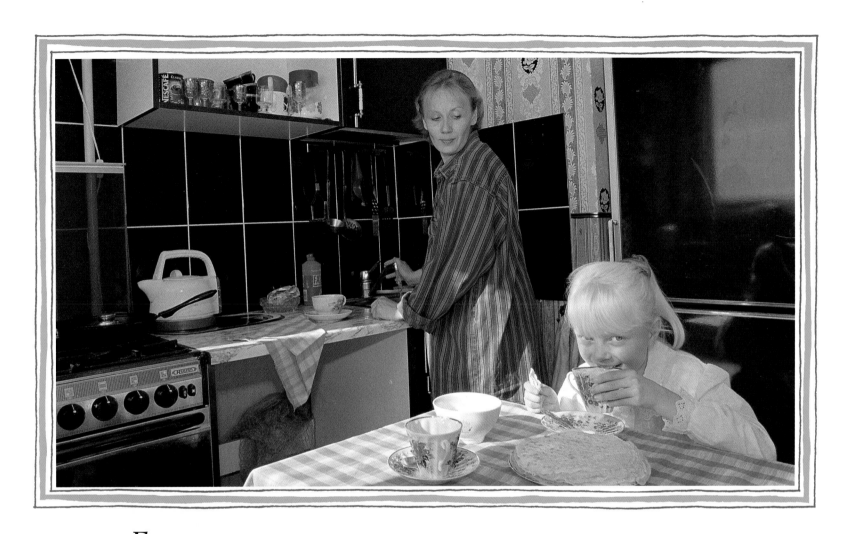

For a treat, Polina's mother has prepared some *bliny* and *smetana* for breakfast today instead of the usual porridge. It's just the two of them as Polina's father has already had to leave for work.

BLINY are traditional Russian pancakes, made out of buck-wheat flour and yeast. They can be served with all sorts of different fillings, like smetana (a kind of sour cream), melted butter, ham or even caviar (fish eggs).

Polina loves reading so she goes to the library whenever she can. This morning she is the first person in the reading hall and she has chosen a brand new book. It still has that fresh inky smell from the printers.

The librarian registers the book in Polina's *formular* (library card). Readers are allowed to keep books for two weeks but Polina likes the look of this one so much, she'll probably finish it in a couple of days.

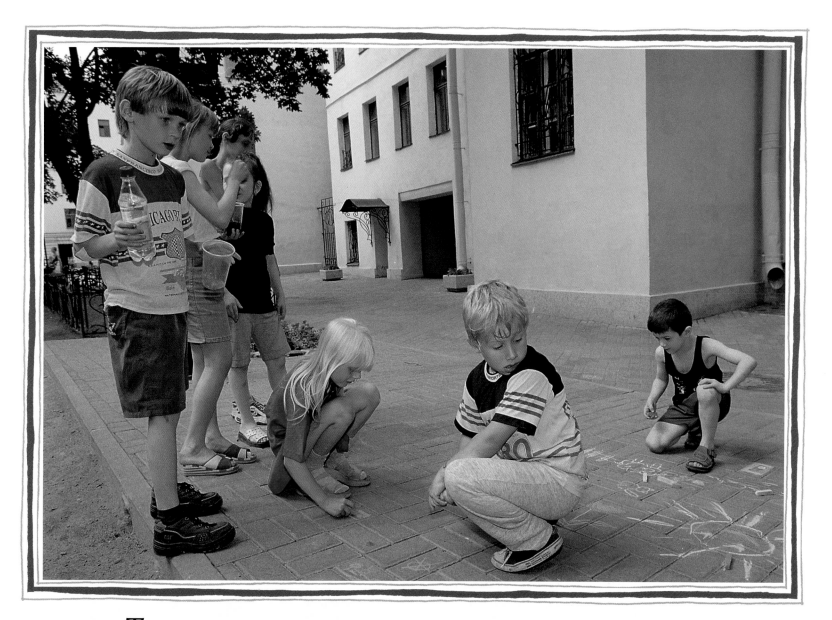

There's still some time before classes start. Polina and her friends
do some chalk drawings on the pavement outside the library.

Polina is never late for school. By 9 o'clock she and her classmates are in the classroom with their textbooks all ready. Before they start, the teacher takes the register and checks everyone's homework.

The first lesson of the day is Russian language. The teacher asks for volunteers to come up to the board, but only the bravest ones in the class put up their hands.

Each lesson lasts for 45 minutes but sometimes that seems too long, so the teacher announces a break to play *slova*.

SLOVA means 'words' in Russian. The idea of this game is to make up as many words as possible using the letters of one very long word, which the teacher chooses.

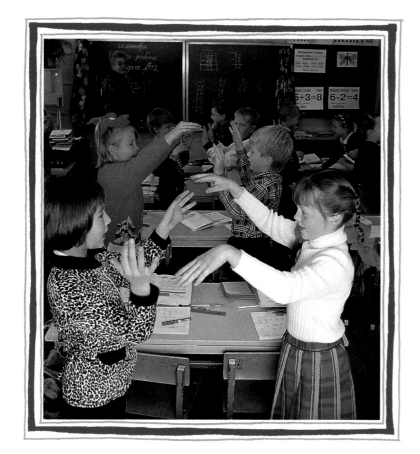

Next they play *ladoshki* (palms).

LADOSHKI The children split into twos and stand facing each other. When the teacher says "go", they push each other's palms to try to make the other person lose their balance. It's not just a game of strength: if you are clever, you can fool your opponent by pretending that you are about to push them really hard, but suddenly pulling back so that they topple into you.

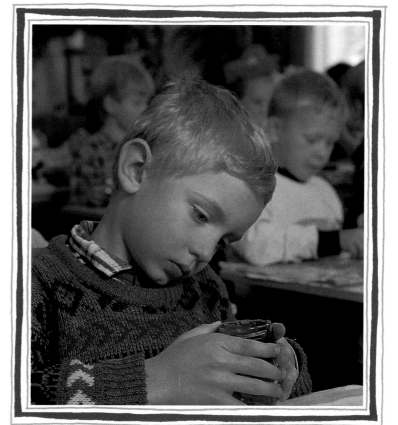

The first lesson after lunch is crafts. Polina's classmate is making a colourful vase out of an old glass jar, plasticine and a mixture of kidney beans and peas.

The last lesson of the day is religious studies. The teacher shows the class slides of churches in different parts of Russia. These people are lighting candles and saying prayers for their families and friends.

The saint in this painting is believed to protect the church and all the people who pray there.

The sound of *kolokola* (bells) can be heard all over Saint Petersburg several times a day.

KOLOKOLA Russian bell-ringing isn't like bell-ringing in Europe, because Russian church bells play rhythms (like drum beats), rather than tunes. Russian bells are also much lighter than European ones, which means one person can play lots of bells at the same time.

11

After school, Polina and her mother catch the tram into the centre of Saint Petersburg. Here they are passing over one of the hundreds of bridges in the city. Sometimes Saint Petersburg gets called 'Northern Venice' because, just like the famous city of Venice in Italy, so many rivers and waterways flow through it.

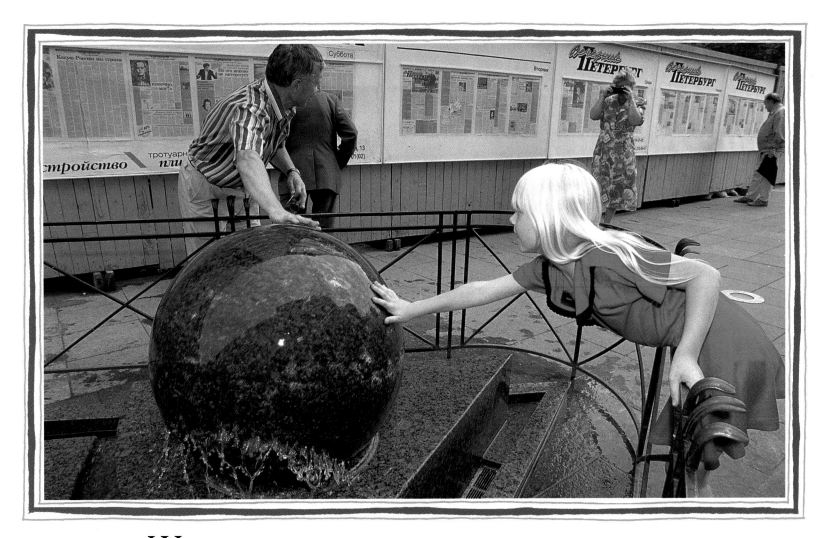

Whenever she walks by this, Polina can't resist playing with it. The stone sphere is supported by a thin layer of water, so even though it is very heavy, Polina can rotate it easily.

13

In one of the squares near *Nevsky Prospekt*, a street artist gives Polina a quick lesson on portrait drawing.

NEVSKY PROSPEKT is the main street of Saint Petersburg. People spend a long time walking along it because there are so many old buildings to admire and interesting shops to visit.

14

Art can be hard work –
Polina decides it's time
for ice-cream!

When her mother
isn't looking, Polina
buys her some flowers
as a present.

Back home, Polina gets together with some of her friends for a game of catch.

They play *klassy* (hopscotch) too.

16

Then Polina and her friend Katya have an idea. They run inside to tell Polina's grandfather about it and he finds them some paper, cotton and some plywood.

When their new kite is ready, Polina, Katya and their friend Hayal, who lives nearby, run back to the park to try it out.

Later on, Polina goes to her theatre group at the local leisure centre.

To warm up, the children play a memory game called *ovetchya golova* (sheep head). The first person to make a mistake gets called "ovetchya golova" by the rest of the group.

Today's rehearsal is the last one before the play will be performed in front of an audience. To wish his cast good luck, the leader of the theatre group has brought in some *arbuz* (watermelon).

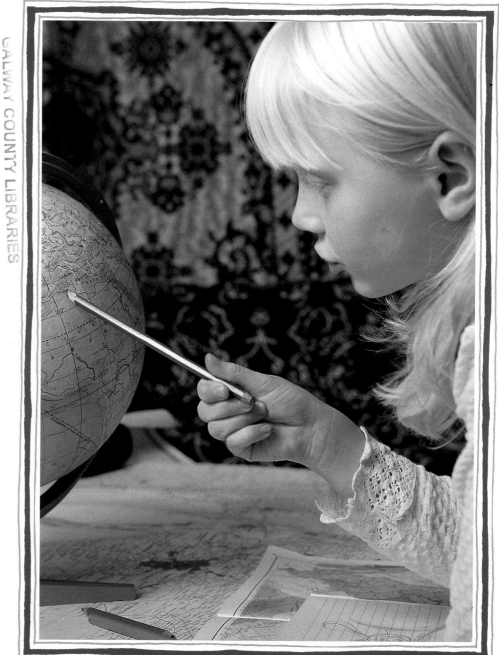

It is late already but Polina has some homework to do before tomorrow. First she has to copy some sentences from her textbook and underline the adjectives in each one.

The second piece of homework is more difficult: Polina has to write a short story about somewhere in Russia she would like to visit. She chooses Lake Baikal, the deepest lake in the world, in an area of Russia called Siberia.

21

When Polina has finished her homework, the family gather around the *samovar* (a kind of water heater) for tea.

SAMOVARS were first made in Russia about a hundred years ago and they are specially designed to boil water quickly and easily. Once the tea has been made, the teapot is put on top of the samovar so that the tea inside stays hot.

Before she goes to bed, Polina's grandma reads her a bedtime story.

Spokoinoi nochi, Polina
(Goodnight, Polina).

MORE ABOUT RUSSIA

Russia is the largest country in the world. It stretches like a giant umbrella from Europe all the way across Asia to America. It's so big that even if you caught a plane, it would take you 10 hours to travel from one end of the country to the other. By train, the same journey would take at least a week, so you would get plenty of time to look out the window and watch the scenery rushing by. Russia has many different kinds of landscape: dry desert in the south-west of the country, large areas of forest in the north, and a vast treeless zone near the north pole (called the 'tundra'), where the ground is frozen solid all year round.

RUSSIA, THE PAST

For hundreds of years Russia was ruled by powerful emperors, called 'tsars' (pronounced 'zars'). But in 1917 two important revolutions took place that changed Russia forever. The first, the February Revolution, was led by a group of Russians who thought the whole system of tsars was unfair: they forced the tsar of the time to give up his power and set up a new government instead. The second, the October Revolution, was organised by the 'Bolsheviks': they didn't like the new government and so they put a different one in its place. After that, Russia became a 'Communist' country and life for ordinary Russian people was often difficult – under the Communist system, they had to get special permission to travel abroad and if they went to the church, or even read books that the Communist rulers didn't approve of, they risked severe punishment.

But these harsh times couldn't last forever, and in 1991 the Communists lost their power. Russia is no longer separate from the rest of the world, and everyday life for the Russian people has changed once again.

RELIGION IN RUSSIA.

Most Russians are Orthodox Christians so Easter is one of the biggest holidays of the year. In almost every home, people make a special onion broth and paint the shells of hard-boiled eggs to give them a beautiful ochre (yellowy-orange) colour. When guests arrive, they are greeted with the exclamation, "Christ has arisen!" and given a painted egg as a present.

PEOPLE IN RUSSIA.

The best thing about Russia is the people that live there. Russian people are full of energy and ideas, which is why there have been so many Russian writers, artists and scientists in history. The Russian writers Leo Tolstoy and Anton Chekhov are famous all over the world. Although they wrote their books and plays a long time ago, their stories can still tell us a lot about the mystery of what it is to be human.

Russians love to read, whether it's Tolstoy, Chekhov or the daily newspaper. On the subway in Moscow in rush hour, you can always see people sandwiched next to each other with their heads buried in a book. In fact, reading in Russia is probably almost as popular as ice-cream eating – and that's saying a lot because Russians are crazy about ice-cream! There are hundreds of ice-cream stalls in every town and people enjoy it even in the depths of *zima* (winter), when the air outside in the streets is as icy cold as the ice-cream itself.

LANGUAGE IN RUSSIA

If you opened up a Russian book, the first thing you would notice is that all the letters are different from the ones used to write English. That's because Russian has a completely different alphabet: English is made up of 26 letters and starts with a, b, c, whereas the Russian alphabet has 32 letters and starts with а, б, в. (The Russian words in *Polina's Day* have been specially written using the English alphabet so that you can read them.)

As well as having a longer alphabet, most Russian words are longer than English ones, which means our books have to be longer too. These long words make it quite difficult to write pop songs in Russian, but they are perfectly suited to the slow melodies of Russian folk music. When you listen to these old songs, it is easy to imagine Russia's vast open spaces and our long, cold winters.

All schoolchildren in Russia learn English because it means they will be able to talk to people from other countries when they are older. We've also borrowed some words from English, especially ones to do with technology, and made them our own – like *kompjuter* and *aeroplan*. I think you can probably guess what they mean!

SOME RUSSIAN WORDS AND PHRASES

privet! (pree-*vyet*) – hello!

dobroye utro (*dob*-row-yeh *uh*-tro) – good morning

Kak dela? (kak de-*lah*) – How are you?

Kotoriy chas? (ko-*tor*-ree chas) – What is the time?

spasibo (spa-*see*-boh) – thank you

do svidania (do svee-*dah*-nyah) – goodbye

THE RUSSIAN WORDS IN THE BOOK

aeroplan – aeroplane

Anton Chekhov – a famous Russian playwright, who was born in 1860 and died in 1904. One of his most well known plays is *The Cherry Orchard*

arbuz – watermelon

bliny – traditional Russian pancakes, which can be served with many different fillings

Bolshevik – the old name for a member of the Russian Communist Party

formular – library card

klassy – hopscotch

kolokola – bells

kompjuter – computer

ladoshki – 'palms', a classroom game

Lake Baikal – a large lake in Siberia

Leo Tolstoy – a famous Russian writer, who was born in 1828 and died in 1910. His two most well known books are *Anna Karenina* and *War and Peace*

Nevsky Prospekt – Nevsky Avenue, the main street in Saint Petersburg

ovetchya golova – 'sheephead', a memory game

Peterburdgets – the name given to people who come from the city of Saint Petersburg

samovar – a special Russian water heater used to make tea and keep it hot

Siberia – a vast region of Russia

slova – 'words', a classroom game

smetana – a kind of sour cream, often served as a filling with bliny

Spokoinoi nochi – Goodnight

tsar – the title that used to be given to Russian emperors

zima – the Russian winter, which lasts from the end of November to the end of March

INDEX